CREATURES
OF THE PARANORMAL

AMERICAN
GHOSTS

Kate Mikoley

T0017334

Enslow Publishing
101 W. 23rd Street
Suite 240
New York, NY 10011
USA

enslow.com

Published in 2020 by Enslow Publishing, LLC
101 W. 23rd Street, Suite 240, New York, NY 10011

Library of Congress Cataloging-in-Publication Data

Names: Mikoley, Kate, author.
Title: American ghosts / Kate Mikoley.
Description: New York : Enslow Publishing, 2020. | Series: Creatures of the paranormal | Includes bibliographical references and index. | Audience: Grades 5-8.
Identifiers: LCCN 2019006394| ISBN 9781978513570 (library bound) | ISBN 9781978513563 (pbk.)
Subjects: LCSH: Ghosts—United States.
Classification: LCC BF1472.U6 M53 2019 | DDC 133.10973—dc23
LC record available at https://lccn.loc.gov/2019006394

Printed in the United States of America

To Our Readers: We have done our best to make sure all websites in this book were active and appropriate when we went to press. However, the author and the publisher have no control over and assume no liability for the material available on those websites or on any websites they may link to. Any comments or suggestions can be sent by email to customerservice@enslow.com.

Portions of this book appeared in *Ghosts in America* by Diane Bailey.

Photo Credits: American Ghosts – Research by Bruce Donnola

Cover and p. 1 (top) Stocksnapper/Shutterstock.com; cover and p. 1 (bottom) Fer Gregory/Shutterstock.com; p. 5 katalinks/Shutterstock.com; p. 8 The History Collection/Alamy Stock Photo; p. 10 Lario Tus/Shutterstock.com; p. 14 Pictures Now/Alamy Stock Photo; p. 16 Zack Frank/Shutterstock.com; p. 17 Iryna Mishyna/Shutterstock.com; pp. 21, 24 Nina Leen/The LIFE Picture Collection/Getty Images; p. 27 Henry Groskinsky/The LIFE Images Collection/Getty Images; p. 30 Album/Alamy Stock Photo; p. 33 MPI/Archive Photos/Getty Images; p. 35 Science & Society Picture Library/Getty Images; p. 38 Bettmann/Getty Images; p. 40 United Archives GmbH/Alamy Stock Photo; p. 42 eddtoro/Shutterstock.com.

CONTENTS

INTRODUCTION

According to a survey from 2009, 18 percent of Americans claim to have seen a ghost. Another poll in 2013 showed that nearly 45 percent of people believe in ghosts, whether they have personally seen one or not. The majority of people may not believe that ghosts are real, but that doesn't mean there is any shortage of fascinating stories out there about them.

Whether they believe it to be true or not, most people have heard a story or two about a haunted hotel or a scary sound coming from an otherwise vacant room. Ghost stories like these are nothing new. For years, people have told tales about those who had died, but who were not quite ready to leave their lives behind. Some ghosts are said to haunt and try to scare living people, while others simply hang around their old homes or places they visited during their time on Earth.

Ghosts are often said to take many forms. Sometimes people say they look as the person would have looked when they were alive. They may be transparent or able to travel through walls or closed doors. To some, they appear to float rather than walk. Occasionally, the ghost is not seen at all, but rather felt or heard, making odd sounds or forcing inanimate objects to move.

Ghosts are often thought to haunt very old buildings or towns because these places are full of history—and many people have likely died there!

Perhaps one reason ghost stories are so popular is that no one really knows the truth for sure. For many, ghost stories are fun, made-up tales for entertainment. Many times, people have claimed to have seen ghosts, but later it came out that they made the whole story up or it was a hoax. However, there have been other reports that have not been so easy to disprove or dismiss. For some people, the simple possibility that ghosts could be real is enough to peak their interest.

The belief that ghosts may exist comes from an idea that dates all the way back to ancient times. The idea is that a person's spirit can be separated from their body. Those who believe in this think that a person's spirit can exist even after that person has died. After the body has died, that spirit becomes the ghost.

Today, even though many people think of ghosts as creatures of the imagination, they have still become a huge part of American culture. They are popular topics in many movies, television shows, and books. Places widely thought to be haunted have become popular tourist destinations. Some people are afraid of ghosts, but others purposely visit haunted sites hoping to have a run-in with a disembodied spirit. In areas all over the country, tourism companies offer ghost tours. On these tours, a guide tells the visitors all about supposed local hauntings. These stories can be appealing even to those who do not believe in ghosts.

1

SOLVED FROM THE GRAVE

It has been said that dead men tell no tales. But those who believe in ghosts may disagree. In fact, some might say that certain ghosts have quite a lot to tell. Some ghosts want to reveal the truth about their lives—and their deaths. In some cases, these ghosts have inspired those still living to search deeper for the truth.

THE REAPPEARING WOMAN

In January 1897, a couple named Edward and Zona Shue lived in Greenbrier County, West Virginia. One cold day, Edward sent eleven-year-old Andy Jones to the Shues' home to find out if Zona needed anything from the store. But Andy did not get a shopping

Zona Shue was found at the bottom of the stairs in her home. After her death, she became known as the Greenbrier Ghost.

list from Zona. Instead, he found her sprawled on the floor. She was dead.

When the local doctor, George Knapp, arrived at the couple's home to examine the body, a seemingly grief-stricken Edward was crying and appeared visibly upset. Knapp wasn't sure how Zona died. He thought he saw bruises on her neck, but he was anxious to get through the situation. He pronounced Zona dead from natural causes.

Zona's mother, Mary Jane Heaster, was suspicious. Her daughter had been married to Edward for only a few months. Mary Jane had never liked him. She wondered whether there was more to the story. But first, she was faced with the sad task of burying her daughter.

Zona's body was laid out for the wake, an event where people gather to say goodbye to the dead. During this time, Edward behaved oddly. He would not allow anyone to get too close to his wife's body. He carefully wrapped a scarf around her neck and insisted on being the only one to arrange the pillows around her head. Still, people noticed that Zona's head seemed "loose."

After the wake, Mary Jane removed the sheet that Zona had rested on in the coffin. It smelled badly, so she washed it. When she did, she said the water in the tub turned red! When she pulled the sheet out, she said it had turned pink. Mary Jane was convinced this was a sign. She believed the mysterious stains were blood and that Zona had not died naturally, but had been murdered!

Mary Jane was convinced that Zona could tell her what had really happened. For the next few weeks, she prayed for her daughter to come to her and reveal the truth.

Mary Jane believed her daughter's death was suspicious from the start. Her prayers were answered when Zona's ghost returned to tell Mary Jane what really happened the day Zona died.

Then one night, the air in the room where Mary Jane slept grew cold. It was not just the chill of winter. It was the cold surrounding the visitor who had appeared—Zona's ghost! Over the course of four nights, Mary Jane reported that Zona returned to her mother and woke her up. She told Mary Jane a terrible story. Zona confided that Edward had not been a good husband. He was often mean to her. On the day of her death, he had flown into a rage just because Zona did not have any meat to cook for his dinner. Then, he attacked her and broke her neck!

As Mary Jane listened in horror, she said Zona's ghost slowly swiveled her head completely around to prove what she was saying. No wonder Edward had not let anyone near Zona's body. If he had, someone might have discovered the true cause of her death. Mary Jane had the proof she needed and she took the evidence to the authorities.

REEXAMINING THE DEATH

Meanwhile, other facts about Edward were discovered. He was new to town, and people had not known him well. It turned out Zona was his third wife. He had reportedly beaten his first wife, and his second wife had also died suddenly. Even if some people

IN THE NEWS

On the day Zona's death was reported in the local newspaper, another interesting article also appeared. This one told about a man in Australia who said he had seen the ghost of a murder victim. Eventually, the man admitted to making it up. He had seen the murder happen but had been threatened into not telling the truth. He thought the lie could help solve the case—and it did.

Some believe Zona's mother read this article and got an idea. They believe she made the story of Zona's ghost up to get people to believe her suspicions that Edward murdered Zona.

did not fully believe Mary Jane's ghost story, there was no doubt that Edward's character was questionable. Many had also noticed his strange behavior after Zona died.

Zona's body was exhumed, or dug up, and examined more closely. Doctors discovered that she had indeed died after someone had choked her. Edward was charged with murder and went to trial. The defense attorney had Mary Jane tell her "ghost story," hoping it would show she was not a reliable witness. The attorney asked her to admit the visions had been dreams, but Mary Jane remained firm. "I am not going to say that; for I am not going to lie," she said. In the end, the jury convicted Edward, and he was sent to prison.

Mary Jane was the only person who saw Zona's ghost, and some think she made the story up to catch Edward for the crime she believed he had committed. Maybe Mary Jane thought that by inventing the ghost story, she would gain the sympathy of other people in the town—and could convince them Edward had murdered Zona.

No one will ever know for sure what really happened. For the twenty years afterward that Mary Jane lived, she stood by her story, and Zona became known as a ghost who helped solve her own murder.

2

STAYING THE NIGHT?

In a 2010 basketball game, the New York Knicks lost badly to the Oklahoma City Thunder. The night before the game, the Knicks stayed at an old Oklahoma City hotel. After the game, some players blamed the loss on the fact that they hadn't slept much because their hotel was haunted! In 2013, a player from the Phoenix Suns staying at the same hotel said when he woke up, his bathtub had mysteriously been filled with water. Ghost sightings at hotels are far from uncommon. Many people have reported seeing ghosts at hotels all over the United States!

EVENING AT THE BROOKDALE

The sounds of clinking glasses and people talking fill the Brookdale Lodge, located in Santa Cruz, California. Music comes from the Fireside Room and the Pool Room. A jukebox is playing in the

In the early 1900s, the dining room at the Brookdale Lodge brought the beauty of the outdoors inside. It even featured a bridge that crossed over the stream.

Mermaid Room. It sounds like a party is going on. The only problem is that the rooms are empty—at least of living people.

So who's making all the noise? Perhaps they are ghosts of past guests, reliving the heyday of the Brookdale. From the 1920s through the 1940s, it was a popular resort where famous people, including President Herbert Hoover (1874–1964) and movie stars such as Mae West (1893–1980), stayed. Songs were even written about the Brookdale.

One of Brookdale's big attractions was the dining room, called the Brookroom. It was built so that a stream, which came down from the surrounding mountains, ran right through the middle of the room. Rocks, trees, and bushes made the room feel like it was part of nature. Tables overlooked the earthy scene, which brought the beauty of the surrounding redwood forests inside. It was a great play area for children—until tragedy struck.

THE GHOST OF A GIRL

The story says that sometime in the 1940s, a six-year-old girl, Sarah Logan, drowned in the Brookroom stream. But it seems Sarah wasn't ready to leave the Brookdale. Employees and guests have spotted a little girl, dressed in a fancy, blue-and-white dress. She is often playing by the fireplace or on the balcony above the dining area. Sometimes the little girl will approach guests. Crying and upset, she will ask them to help her find her mother. The guests are happy to help. Usually they turn away for a moment to look for the missing mother. But when they turn back, the little girl is gone. Employees are convinced this little girl is Sarah. Perhaps it is even more frightening that the girl does not appear particularly "ghostly." According to reports, she was "very clear, like a whole person." That is, until the people watching her saw her ghost run through a solid wall!

As Sarah looks for her mother, her mother may also be looking for her. Diners in the Brookroom have reported seeing a woman floating above the creek, as if she was standing on a bridge that is no longer there. Some people believe this mysterious woman could be Sarah's mother. In addition, the smell of gardenias takes

HAUNTING HOTELS

Haunted hotels are a pop-
ular theme in movies and
books. In 1977, Stephen
King released a book called
The Shining, which was later
made into a movie. It told of
a haunted hotel.

While the hotel in the
book was fictional, it was
based on a real place King
had stayed—The Stanley
Hotel in Estes Park, Colorado.
Many guests have reported
seeing ghosts at the hotel,
namely that of F. O. Stanley,
the hotel's original owner,
and his wife, Flora. Some
say they've seen the hotel's piano playing all by itself. It's believed Flora often
played the piano during her life!

The original owners aren't the only ghosts
reported at the Stanley hotel. Other
accounts tell of a haunting housekeeper and
mysterious sounds of children laughing.

over the room at night—even though that particular flower isn't
planted anywhere in the Brookdale.

MORE HAUNTINGS

Some people believe Sarah's death changed the fates and fortunes
of the Brookdale. Throughout the 1940s and 1950s, it became a
much less glamorous place. It is said that criminals and gangsters
started to fill the Brookdale's rooms. Perhaps they also filled the

Some accounts say that Sarah was playing near the stream and fell and hit her head on the surrounding rocks, leading her to drown. Her ghost is said to still roam the Brookdale.

places beneath it. Rumors spread that bodies were buried in the secret rooms and passageways that had been built below the lodge. It's said there is a haunted meat locker, which is now sealed off. Some believe mobsters may have murdered their victims there because their screams could not be heard through the thick walls.

Room 46 in the Brookdale seems to be particularly haunted. An employee who lived in the room reported that she would see objects flying across the room at night. Once she said she even felt someone sit down next to her and touch her. She also saw several people, such as ballroom dancers who seemed to be enjoying a night of entertainment. But some of the ghosts seen at the Brookdale were much scarier, such as a man with his face badly cut, and another with his eye falling out of its socket. Perhaps these were victims from the Brookdale's period as a gangster hangout.

One spirit is said to be a lumberjack named George. Some think he could be from the lodge's early days as a lumber mill in the late 1800s. It's said that he can be heard in the conference room, where doors sometimes slam for no reason. Occasionally, people see him behind the lodge, in a spot where wood was chopped to feed the fireplaces.

Something about the Brookdale seems to make ghosts stick around. Over the years, the hotel's owners have called in psychics to investigate the ghosts. They have identified forty-nine different spirits! The Brookdale seems to be open to all—even the dead!

3

JUST POPPING BY

A ccording to some stories, there are some ghosts who are quiet and shy. They don't want to hurt or bother anyone. But there are others who want to be noticed. It becomes impossible to ignore these kinds of ghosts. The word "poltergeist" comes from the German words *poltern,* meaning "to knock or rattle," and *geist*, meaning "ghost." It makes sense, then, that the word "poltergeist" refers to a noisy ghost.

GHOSTLY BOTTLES

It was just an ordinary day in early February 1958 when thirteen-year-old Lucille Herrmann and her twelve-year-old brother James came home from school to their house on Long Island, New York. But soon after their arrival, things got weird. All over the house, tops started popping off bottles! From bleach in the basement and starch in the kitchen to shampoo and medicine in the bathroom, lids were popping off everywhere. There was even a bottle of holy water in the master bedroom that lost its top. The Herrmann children and their mother were mystified. When Mr. Herrmann got home from work that evening, he had no explanation either. The tops of the bottles were not the kind they could easily come off. They were the kind that screwed on and off.

At first, the family believed the strange incident was just a one-time event. They decided not to worry about it too much. But then, a few days later, it happened again. Now Mr. Herrmann was suspicious. James was good at science. Mr. Herrmann suspected he might be pulling an elaborate prank. More bottles exploded a few days later. Some of them even moved by themselves as he watched. Mr. Herrmann accused James of playing a trick, but James denied it. After investigating, Mr. Herrmann became convinced his son was innocent. Maybe there was a logical explanation, but the Herrmanns could not find it. It seemed the house was being bothered by a very troublesome ghost.

ASKING FOR HELP

Mr. Herrmann decided to call in outside help. He started with the police. They were skeptical at first, but when the detective on the case, Joseph Tozzi, witnessed the strange activity himself, he decided the Herrmanns had a real problem. However, he had no idea what was causing the disturbances. Next, the Herrmanns called in a priest to bless the house. This did not stop the popping either.

In the beginning, Mr. Herrmann thought that maybe his son James, shown here, had put something inside the bottles to make the caps pop off.

ARSON OR POLTERGEIST?

During the summer of 1948, hundreds of fires broke out in one home in Macomb, Illinois. A thirteen-year-old named Wanet McNeill lived in the home with her father—and perhaps a poltergeist. Wanet was upset she had to live there after her parents' divorce. The fires started as little spots on the wallpaper of the home. They would then burst into flames. Neighbors even reported seeing this happen. But eventually, officials stated that Wanet had started the fires herself. They said she confessed, but some still believe the fires were the workings of a poltergeist!

Meanwhile, the poltergeist, who had been nicknamed "Popper," was branching out from bottles. Figurines and dishes were lifted from their resting places and hovered in the air. Then, the poltergeist began hurling objects several feet across the room. The items got bigger and more dangerous. While James was doing his homework one evening, his record player flew across the room. A globe zoomed down the hallway, almost hitting Detective Tozzi, who was in the house at the time. A bookcase fell over, too.

The incidents captured the attention of the media. Newspaper and television reporters showed up to find out what was going on. People from all over the country wrote to the Herrmanns, suggesting explanations and solutions. One person thought it must be

Martians. Another decided it was Russian troops, tunneling under Long Island in order to attack New York. There was no shortage of strange ideas people had for the mysterious happenings.

Many natural causes were investigated as well. Detective Tozzi ruled out underground streams causing a strange magnetic field, radio waves, sonic booms from nearby aircraft, changes in the underground water level, and a downdraft from the fireplace. By now, the Herrmanns were ready for anyone's help. That's when they enlisted the help of two men from Duke University, who specialized in parapsychology.

A CHILD'S POWER?

Dr. J. Gaither Pratt and Dr. William Roll had been studying cases in which people could supposedly move objects without actually touching them, called psychokinesis, or PK. Because it is thought that poltergeist activity often occurs around growing children or teenagers, some people think it has to do with the growing energies, which the children are unable to express otherwise. Without necessarily meaning to, some believe the children apply their energy to the objects around them, making them move.

The doctors wondered if this might be the case at the Herrmanns' house. Most of the incidents had occurred when James was in the room or nearby. One night, when the family spent a night away from home and left the house with Detective Tozzi, nothing happened.

Psychologists did determine that James had some hostility toward his parents. Even if James was somehow causing the activity, the

In addition to poltergeists, Dr. J. Gaither Pratt, shown here talking to James Herrmann, also studied other concepts related to the paranormal. A collection of some of his work is stored at Duke University.

paranormal researchers did not believe he was doing it on purpose. Pratt told a reporter, "The family was much too shaken for it to be a colossal hoax."

On March 10, a little more than a month after the supposed poltergeist arrived, it left. It popped the top off one last bleach bottle as a final goodbye. No one—from plumbers to police to paranormal psychologists—ever figured out for sure what caused the activity. The Herrmanns were just glad that whatever it was had decided not to "pop by" anymore!

WHAT ARE YOU LOOKING FOR?

If someone loses something important, they probably go back to where they lost it and search for it. Sometimes, ghosts do the same thing—and they might not leave until they find what they've been looking for!

GUNNING DOWN A GHOST

In 1916, Robert Lamont moved into a place called Summerwind located in northern Wisconsin. He had big plans. He converted the former fishing lodge into a mansion for his family where they lived for several years. Then, one evening when Lamont was eating in the kitchen, the door leading to the basement began to shake. Suddenly,

Summerwind, shown here in the early 1980s, was located on the shores of West Bay Lake in Wisconsin. It was said to be home to numerous hauntings before it was abandoned.

it opened, and Lamont saw a man standing there. According to some accounts, the man even tried to attack Lamont.

Lamont pulled out his gun and fired two shots. Perhaps Lamont did not realize at first that his opponent was not a living man, but rather a ghost. But he soon found out because his gun did not affect the ghost. The figure was not killed, or even wounded. In fact, he wasn't there at all. Only the bullet holes in the door remained. Convinced that his house was haunted, Lamont moved out soon after.

For the next few decades, things were fairly quiet at Summerwind. Several different people owned the house, but it cost too much money to keep up. Besides, some said the house gave them a creepy feeling. One by one, everyone gave up on Summerwind.

Then, in the early 1970s, Arnold and Ginger Hinshaw moved in with their children. If ghosts had been sleeping at Summerwind, the Hinshaws woke them up. The paranormal activity began almost immediately. Voices belonging to no one came from empty rooms. Shadows from people who weren't there crept down the hallways. Windows and doors would be found open when they had been left closed. Several times, the family saw a floating image of a woman. Nonetheless, they decided to try to live with the ghosts.

But the hauntings eventually took their toll on the Hinshaws. Arnold's behavior turned strange and was scaring the rest of his family. He began playing the organ in a frenzy. He had a nervous breakdown. Ginger was also not doing well. She tried to commit suicide. Eventually, Arthur got treatment for his mental health issues, while Ginger and the children moved in with her parents. But Ginger had not told her parents exactly what had happened, and her father, Raymond, decided to convert the house into a hotel and restaurant. When Ginger found out, Raymond later wrote, she was horrified and warned him against it. She told him, "There is a presence there. Something powerful and evil."

MORE WEIRD ACTIVITY

Even after being warned, Raymond decided to continue with his plans and began renovating Summerwind. As Ginger had feared, the ghosts came back. Raymond's wife, Marie, felt unsettled by the house. She felt as if someone was watching her. Raymond's son, Karl, also reported having strange experiences when he was alone at the house.

As work on the house started, the weird activity continued. The workmen's tools disappeared, and the workmen, too, reported feeling uneasy in the house. Many of them refused to come to work. Even creepier was the fact that the house seemed to change sizes. Raymond would measure rooms and then find the next day that

HAUNTINGS AT THE WHITE HOUSE

It's been said that ghosts haunt even the president's home. Former presidents, including Abraham Lincoln, Thomas Jefferson, Andrew Jackson, and John Tyler, supposedly haunt different areas of the White House. Perhaps they are searching for something they left behind in the building they once all called home.

Another White House ghost goes by the name "the Thing." This spirit is that of an unknown teenage boy. People have reported feeling a slight force on their shoulder, as if the Thing is looking over their shoulder, trying to look at whatever they're doing.

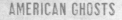
18 9 c

Capt: JONATHAN CARVER.

From the Original Picture in the possession of J.C. Lettsom M.D.

Published as the Act directs by R. Stewart, N.º 287 near G.ª Turnstile Holborn, Nov. 16, 1780.

TRAVELS

THROUGH THE

INTERIOR PARTS

OF

NORTH AMERICA,

IN THE

YEARS 1766, 1767, and 1768.

BY J. CARVER, ESQ.

CAPTAIN OF A COMPANY OF PROVINCIAL
TROOPS DURING THE LATE
WAR WITH FRANCE.

ILLUSTRATED WITH COPPER PLATES,
COLOURED.

THE THIRD EDITION.

To which is added, SOME ACCOUNT OF THE
AUTHOR, AND A COPIOUS INDEX.

LONDON:

Printed for C. DILLY, in the Poultry; H. PAYNE, in
Pall-mall; and J. PHILLIPS, in George-Yard,
Lombard-Street.

M DCC LXXXI.

Jonathan Carver's book *Travels Through the Interior Parts of North America, in the Years 1766, 1767, and 1768*, gave a detailed account of his journeys.

they were an entirely different size. There were even photographs, taken only a few minutes apart, that showed different dimensions.

Raymond claimed to know what was going on. He said the ghost of Jonathan Carver had visited him in a dream. Carver was an eighteenth-century explorer who traveled with Sioux Indians and later wrote a book about his experiences. The editor for his book, along with some of Carver's heirs, later said that Carver had received a land deed, signed by the Sioux Indian chiefs. This deed would have given him a large amount of land in Wisconsin, but no one could prove the story was true.

Raymond said that Carver told him the land deed was buried in the foundation of Summerwind. Raymond concluded the house's hauntings were a result of Carver searching for the deed and trying to scare off anyone who got in his way. Of course, no one could ever prove this story either. People looked, but no one ever found a deed in the foundation. Skeptics think Raymond invented the Carver ghost story to increase business at his future resort.

However, his plans were never finished, and Summerwind never became a resort. In 1988, lightning struck the house and it burned to the ground. If Summerwind's ghosts were trying to keep people away, they got their wish. Today, nothing remains of Summerwind but the chimney, the foundation, and the haunting ghost stories.

5

MOVING ALONG

Some ghosts aren't interested in staying in one place. They don't want to just haunt the same old house forever. Instead, they move around.

A Texas man named Brit Bailey wanted to be buried as he had lived—standing up! He had spent his life traveling about the Texas range—and he didn't think dying was any excuse to stop. Since his death, he's been seen roaming the prairie. Maybe for ghosts like Bailey, it's hard to leave the place in which they spent so much of their lives. Or maybe, they just prefer to always be on the move.

RIDING AWAY

Settlers heading west on the Oregon Trail, exhausted from weeks of hard travel, likely welcomed the sight of Fort Laramie in Wyoming. Fort Laramie was established in 1834 as a fur trading post. Later, it became an important protective place for the US military during

Fort Laramie, shown here about 1845 in this painting by W. H. Jackson, was fairly small at only about 100 feet by 80 feet (30.5 meters by 24.4 meters). But it was a central place for fur trade in the area.

military during the wars of the nineteenth century. The fort was located in the middle of hard, dangerous land.

When Fort Laramie was part of the American Fur Company, the agent in charge brought his daughter to live with him. She was a sophisticated city girl, educated in high-class schools on the East Coast. She was also a skilled equestrian. She loved to take her favorite black horse on long rides around the grounds of the trading post. She was eager to explore.

The girl's father, however, worried about her safety. He told the men who worked for him to watch over her. He also warned her not to leave the post by herself. Beyond the boundaries of the post were all kinds of dangers. The landscape of Wyoming was unforgiving. If one became lost, they might not find their way back home so easily.

Perhaps the girl was stubborn or wanted to rebel against her father. Or perhaps she simply longed for the freedom of riding in the open hills. Either way, she defied his orders to stay close to home. One day, when he was away on business, she left the post. Her father's men chased after her, but she got away from them—forever.

Hours passed, then days. When the girl did not return, her father searched for her, hoping to find answers. Had the girl been captured or murdered? Had she been killed in a bad fall or become hopelessly lost and starved to death? No one would ever know. No one ever saw the girl again—at least not alive.

RIDING ONCE AGAIN

About twenty years after the girl disappeared, James Allison, a lieutenant with the US military, reported for duty at Fort Laramie. One afternoon, when he was out hunting, he became separated from the rest of his group. He called out, but no one answered. Then he saw a horse galloping toward him. However, the rider was not one of the men he had been hunting with. Instead, it was a woman dressed in a striking green riding habit. As she rode past him, she touched a jeweled riding whip to the horse. The pair kept moving.

Lieutenant Allison chased the mysterious woman, but he was not able to catch her. When he came over a small hill, he saw that she and her horse were gone. Lieutenant Allison also saw that the horse

A riding habit, shown here on the right, is the kind of
clothing a woman would wear while horseback riding.
At the time, it included a jacket and long skirt.

In Abbeville, Alabama, there's a story of a hands-on ghost who is responsible for making sure countless children return home by the time their parents told them to be. The tale says that Huggin' Molly wanders the streets of Abbeville, but only those kids out past curfew can see her. If she sees them, the seven-foot-tall (two-meter-tall) figure runs up to them, hugs them, and screams in their ear. Some say it's just a story parents use to make sure their kids return home on time, but most people don't want to be the ones to test that theory!

had left no tracks behind. There was no sign of either the woman or the horse. It was as if they had never been there at all. He realized that he had not heard any hoofbeats either. His dog also seemed upset, perhaps sensing a ghostly presence as well. That evening, back at the post, he told his commanding officer what he had seen. The officer was not surprised. He confirmed, "You have seen our Lady in Green. She appears near the fort about every seven years, and she means no harm."

Lieutenant Allison's curiosity was sparked. He began to ask around to find out more. He spoke to a woman who lived near the fort. She reported that she had seen the girl leave on her "fatal ride," and described the girl's clothing just as Lieutenant Allison had seen it. The woman also confirmed that others in the area had seen her. Years later, he heard some cowboys talking about seeing the ghostly horse and rider. Reported sightings continued late into the twentieth century. Whatever her true fate was, many believe the Lady in Green finally got her chance to ride free.

6

GHOSTS EVERYWHERE

With ghosts being such a popular part of American culture, it can be hard to tell what's thought to be real and what's just entertainment. Often, the ghost stories told in movies, books, and television are based on stories people claim to have experienced with ghosts. Whether fact or fiction, ghosts are as popular today as ever.

COMMUNICATING WITH THE DEAD

Although ghosts are nothing new, they have not always been as accepted in society as they are today. Years ago, people might have believed in ghosts, or they might not have, but either way they did not go around talking about it. That began to change around the 1850s. A philosophy called spiritualism began to take hold. Its followers believed people could communicate with the dead, and they actively tried to do so.

This illustration shows a nineteenth-century séance. A séance is a meeting in which a medium tries to contact a spirit. Those attending usually sit in a circle and there is often little or no light in the room.

Mediums are people who claim to be skilled in summoning and communicating with spirits. Thousands of mediums started working in the United States in the 1800s. Some wanted to help people talk to ghosts. Others probably just wanted to make some money. As this idea that people could communicate with the dead became widespread, it became profitable.

Without a doubt, many mediums were fakes. Leah, Margaret, and Kate Fox were three sisters who lived in New York. They claimed to be able to communicate with ghosts, and many people sought out their services. They had successful careers as mediums for many years before confessing that their talents were just an act.

Despite the acts of fraud, the New England Spiritualist Association estimated that there were two million believers in the United States. In 1854, a senator from Illinois presented a petition to Congress asking the government to "investigate communications from the dead." Not everyone bought into the movement though. In Alabama, a law was passed to stop people from making a public display of being a medium. Nonetheless, the spiritualism movement in the United States was strong until about the 1920s, when it finally began to fade.

GHOSTS IN THE MEDIA

Ghosts continue to thrive in literature. In *The Graveyard Book* by Neil Gaiman, the main character, Nobody Owens, is raised in a graveyard by ghosts. The arrangement works out well for him. His foster parents teach him some handy ghostly tricks that help him defeat his enemies.

In J. K. Rowling's *Harry Potter* series, ghosts wander down the halls and through the walls at Hogwarts School of Witchcraft and Wizardry. Each house at Hogwarts even has its own ghost mascot. Rowling does not make her ghosts particularly mysterious or scary. Instead, they are treated like regular characters who just happen to be dead.

Many popular movies have also featured ghosts. In the 1999 movie *The Sixth Sense*, a young boy is frightened by the ghosts he sees. However, he is encouraged to talk to them, and eventually he realizes that they are simply spirits who need help settling their business in life before they can move on. *ParaNorman* is a 2012 animated movie in which the main character can speak to ghosts. Most people don't believe him, but he has to use his strange ability to save his town from a curse.

GHOSTBUSTERS

In 1984, a movie called *Ghostbusters* told the comedic story of a group of men who started a business hunting down ghosts. The movie was quite a success, and in 1989, a second movie, *Ghostbusters II*, came out. In 2016, a new *Ghostbusters* movie was released. The 2016 film stars four women who started their own ghost-catching team. As in the earlier movies, the team is tasked with capturing a number of ghosts.

The original *Ghostbusters* movie starred (*from left to right*) Ernie Hudson, Dan Aykroyd, Bill Murray, and Harold Ramis as members of the ghost-hunting team.

In the 1980s, three *Poltergeist* movies came out. These were scarier, as the ghosts involved had some sinister motivations. In 2015, a new *Poltergeist* movie was released. Several other recent horror movies have featured ghosts who are clearly out to terrorize their victims.

Ghosts have floated onto the small screen as well. In recent years, many reality shows have taken on the topic of ghosts—and looking for them. *Ghost Hunters* was a popular show that ran from 2004 until 2016. The stars of the show visited reportedly haunted places to investigate the reports of ghost activity.

IN SEARCH OF A GHOST

Though the *Ghostbusters* movies are fictional comedies, many real-life ghost hunters take their jobs very seriously. Across the United States, there are dozens of organizations devoted to investigating paranormal activity. Unlike the mediums of more than a century ago, however, these people do not rely on candlelight and a creepy atmosphere. Instead, they use scientific instruments that can pick up actual physical changes in the environment, such as electro-magnetic fields or cold spots in the atmosphere. Some people believe these things can indicate the presence of ghosts.

The stars of *Ghost Hunters* are part of a group called The Atlantic Paranormal Society (TAPS). This is a team of paranormal investigators who look into stories of ghosts and hauntings. Shows such as *Ghost Hunters* are supposed to be based in reality. However, they have regularly drawn criticism for using questionable scientific methods or for outright making up some of the stories. In addition, some

A member of the Brooklyn Paranormal Society checks the equipment before the team sets off to investigate the possible presence of paranormal activity in Long Island, New York.

people think the sensational aspect of television makes studying the paranormal seem silly.

Still, there are many people who devote their time and skills to studying supernatural phenomena. They try to understand not only why the ghosts are there, but how some people can see them and even communicate with them. It is possible ghost hunting television shows are only a fad, but ghost stories themselves have been around for as long as people have been telling stories. Whether ghosts are real or not, the love for these kinds of tales is not likely to go away any time soon!

BIBLIOGRAPHY

Atlas Obscura. "The Stanley Hotel." Retrieved February, 5, 2019 (https://www.atlasobscura.com/places/the-stanley-hotel-estes-park-colorado).

Birnes, William J., and Joel Martin. *The Haunting of America: From the Salem Witch Trials to Harry Houdini*. New York, NY: Tom Doherty Associates, 2009.

Dickey, Colin. *Ghostland: An American History in Haunted Places*. New York, NY: Viking, 2016.

Frank, Adam. "If Dark Matter Can't Be Seen, What About Ghosts?" NPR.org. September 13, 2016. Retrieved February 5, 2019 (https://www.npr.org/sections/13.7/2016/09/13/493725999/if-dark-matter-cant-be-seen-what-about-ghosts).

Hawes, Jason, Grant Wilson, and Michael Jan Friedman. *Ghost Hunting: True Stories of Unexplained Phenomena from The Atlantic Paranormal Society*. New York, NY: Simon & Schuster, 2007.

Lipka, Michael. "18% of Americans Say They've Seen a Ghost." Pewresearch.org. October 30, 2015. Retrieved February 5, 2019 (http://www.pewresearch.org/fact-tank/2015/10/30/18-of-americans-say-theyve-seen-a-ghost).

MontereyBay.org. "Brookdale Lodge: Haunted or Not?" Retrieved February 5, 2019 (http://montereybay.org/haunted-ghost-brookdale-lodge.html).

Norman, Michael, and Beth Scott. *Historic Haunted America*. New York, NY: Tom Doherty Associates, 2007.

Sceurman, Mark, and Mark Moran. *Weird Hauntings*. New York, NY: Sterling Publishing, 2006.

Steiger, Brad. *Real Ghosts, Restless Spirits, and Haunted Places*. Canton, MI: Visible Ink Press, 2003.

Taylor, Troy. "The Greenbrier Ghost: A Tale from Haunted West Virginia." PrairieGhosts.com. Retrieved February 5, 2019 (https://www.prairieghosts.com/shue.html).

Taylor, Troy. "Popper the Poltergeist: Strange Happenings on New York's Long Island." PrairieGhosts.com. Retrieved February 5, 2019 (http://www.prairieghosts.com/popper.html).

Taylor, Troy. "Summerwind: Wisconsin's Most Haunted House." PrairieGhosts.com. Retrieved February 5, 2019 (http://www.prairieghosts.com/summer.html).

Taylor, Troy. *Weird Illinois*. New York, NY: Sterling Publishing Co, 2005.

GLOSSARY

disembodied Not having or not attached to a body.

equestrian A person who is skilled at riding horses.

fraud A deceitful action or person.

heir A person who inherits money or property from someone who dies.

heyday The period of time when something is at its best or most popular.

inanimate Not living or able to move on its own.

paranormal Something that is outside the realm of normality and cannot be explained through science.

parapsychology The study of mental phenomena that cannot be explained through science.

phenomena Things that occur and are typically unusual or hard to understand or believe.

poltergeist A type of ghost that moves objects and makes a lot of noise.

psychokinesis The power to move objects using the mind.

transparent See-through.

vacant Empty.

FURTHER READING

BOOKS

Chandler, Matt. *Famous Ghost Stories of North America*. North Mankato, MN: Capstone Press, 2019.

McCollum, Sean. *Handbook to Ghosts, Poltergeists, and Haunted Houses*. North Mankato, MN: Capstone Press, 2017.

Vale, Jenna, and Graham Watkins. *Tracking Ghosts and Hauntings*. New York, NY: Rosen Publishing, 2018.

Wood, Alix. *Ghostly Prisons*. New York, NY: Gareth Stevens Publishing, 2017.

WEBSITES

DKfindout! Real Ghosts? Scary Stories From History!

www.dkfindout.com/us/explore/real-ghosts-scary-stories-from-history/

Check out fascinating stories about ghosts throughout history.

History.com: History of Ghost Stories

www.history.com/topics/halloween/historical-ghost-stories

Find out more information on ghosts and haunted places.

The White House Historical Association

www.whitehousehistory.org/press-room/press-fact-sheets/white-house-ghost-stories

Read about the ghost stories of the White House.

INDEX